Do nothing

Manu Won Jin

Do nothing

Loi n°49-956 du 16 juillet 1949 sur les publications destinées à
la jeunesse, modifiée par la loi n°2011-525 du 17 mai 2011.

© 2023, Manu Won Jin

Édition : BoD – Books on Demand, info@bod.fr
Impression : BoD – Books on Demand, In de Tarpen 42, Norderstedt (Allemagne)
Impression à la demande
ISBN : 978-2-3221-5804-1
Dépôt légal : Mars 2023

To my Kindergarten students
who meditate with me every day

Hey you!

Yes, you who is reading a book!

Have you ever tried to do nothing? Let's try! Try to do nothing.

Hey, you just put your book away. But you're not doing nothing! I can see that you're eating.

You're moving your feet now! Come on, just try to do nothing at all.

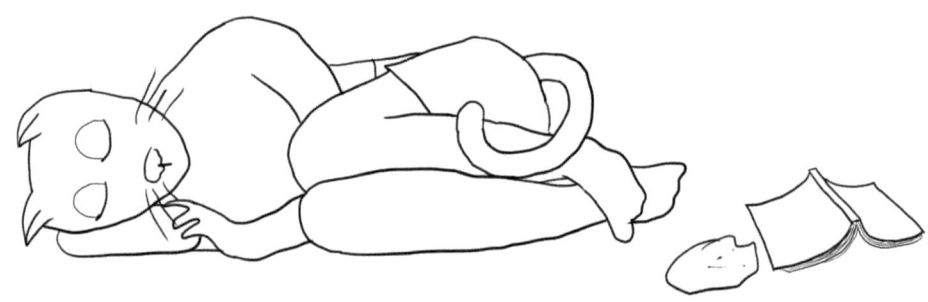

Hey, you're not doing nothing: you're sleeping!

Sleeping and doing nothing are not the same! Just sit and try to do nothing.

Ohhh, but your body is all twisted here. You are leaning to one side! If you lean, you're not doing nothing. To do nothing, you have to keep your body straight.

I said straight. Not uptight like a robot!

Stop moving your eyes.

You don't need to ever do those big eyes. Just stay normal, stay neutral.

Ahhh... Here we are. Good!

Oops, careful: you just smiled!

And now you have an angry face! Come on, just stay normal! Just do NOTHING.

Ah-ha... Now you are doing nothing. See, it's possible to do nothing!

Sometimes we do nothing because we don't know what to do. But some other times, we do nothing because we just want to do nothing. There are even people who sometimes go join other people just to do nothing together.

Doing nothing on purpose is called "to meditate." To meditate means to do meditation. And to do meditation means to do nothing on purpose.

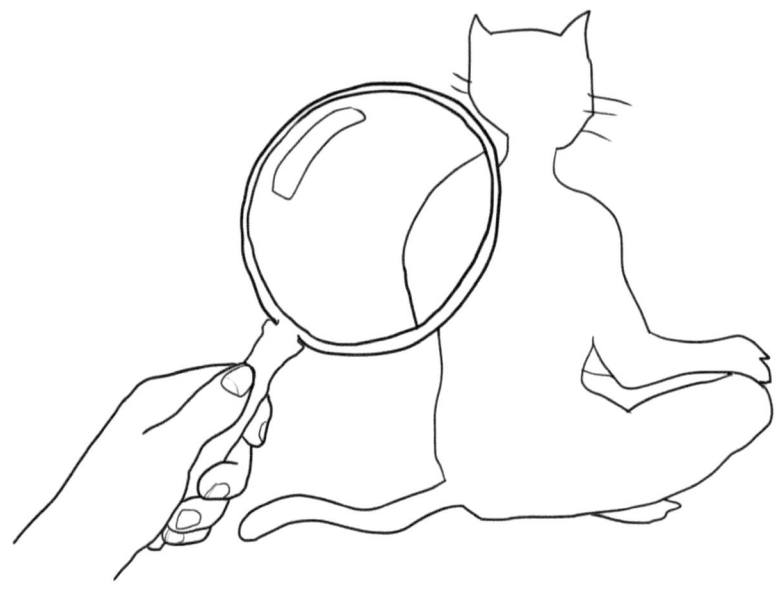

But what does our body do when we do nothing? Let's see...

Try to do nothing for 10 seconds. Do your ears still work? Can you still hear when you do nothing?

Yes! Even when we do nothing, our ears keep hearing by themselves!

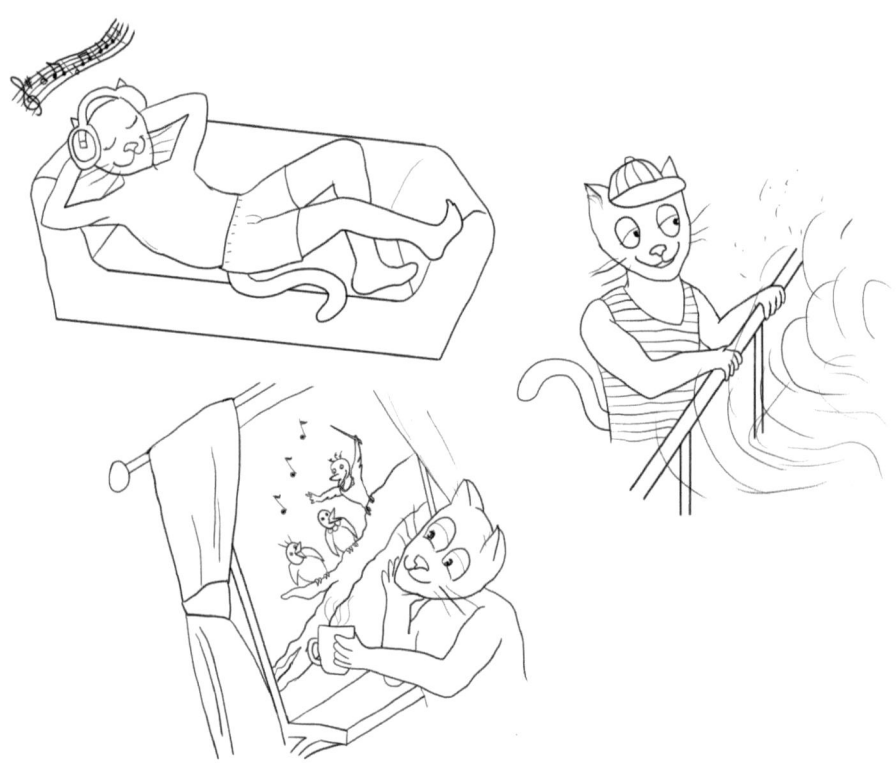

Usually when we hear sounds, we react. It means that there are sounds that we like and sounds that we don't like. Myself, for example, I like to hear nice music, I like to hear the birds, I like to hear the waves of the water...

But I really don't like hearing a slamming door, or the noise of road work outside, or the noise of a breaking plate...

It makes me want to go... *AHHHHH !!!!!*

But when we do nothing, it's different. When we do nothing, we can let our ears hear without reacting. We just say to ourselves "Oh-oh! There is a sound." Oh-oh, singing birds here... Oh-oh, slamming door there... Oh-oh, road work outside...

Now, try again to do nothing for 10 seconds. Do your eyes still work? Can you still see when you do nothing?

Yes! When we do nothing, our eyes keep seeing. It's like the ears: when we do nothing, our eyes keep working by themselves.

Usually when we see with our eyes, we react. There are things we like to see and there are things we don't like to see. Myself, for example, I like to see a beautiful landscape.

But I don't like to see dirt or dust. It makes me cringe!

But when we do nothing, it's different. When we do nothing, we can let our eyes see without reacting. We just say to ourselves "Oh-oh, there is something." Oh-oh, there is dirt... Oh-oh, there is dust...

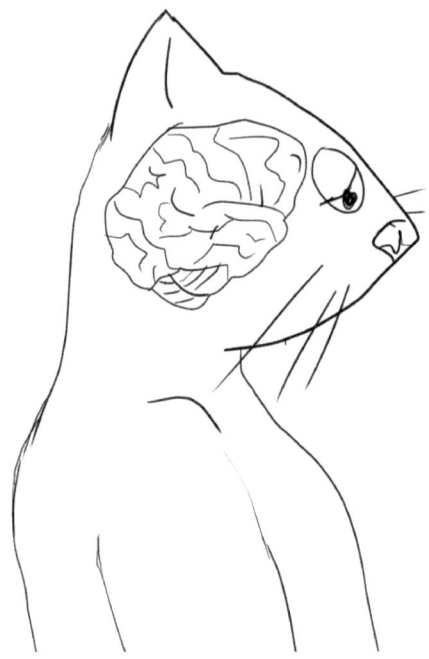

Isn't it funny? When we do nothing, our ears and our eyes keep working. It's normal, and actually there are many other things that our body keeps doing when we do nothing. Because they are things that our body does alone, by itself.

By the way, do you know what our head does when we do nothing?

In your head, there are always many things happening. When you are thinking of a friend, or of your parents or of an animal, all this thinking is happening inside your head. Your head is full of thoughts.

Thoughts make stories in your head. But since we are so used to it, most of the time we don't even notice that we are thinking.

When we do nothing, our head keeps thinking by itself! But the difference is that, when we do nothing, we have time to notice what our head is thinking of. We have time to say to ourselves, "Oh, my head is thinking of something." Oh, my head is thinking of my friends... Oh, my head is thinking of my grandma.. Oh, my head is thinking of my favorite meal... Oh, my head is thinking of my Halloween costume...

Does our body move by itself when we do nothing?

When we do nothing, we are able to stop moving our arms, stop moving our legs, stop moving our hands and fingers, stop moving our head... But is our entire body really still?

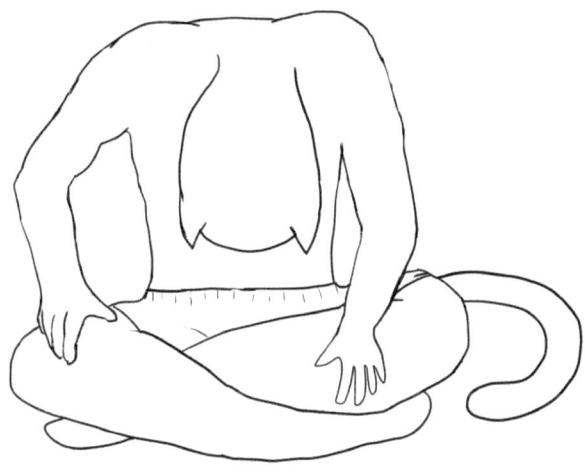

Let's see... Try to do nothing for 20 seconds while watching your belly. Did you see? Your belly moves by itself! It's totally normal! It's because, even when you do nothing, your body keeps breathing. It means that there is air coming inside your body and then going outside of it through your nose and mouth.

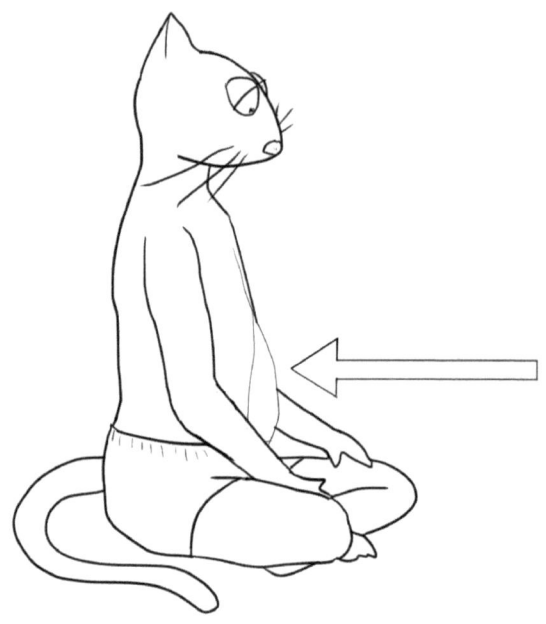

When the air comes in, it goes in your body all the way down toward your belly. When it gets there, it makes your belly inflate a little. Then when the air goes out, your belly deflates. That's why your belly is like a little balloon: it goes out, and then goes in, and then goes out again, and then goes in again, and that never stops!

Usually, we don't even notice that we are breathing. But when we are doing nothing, we have time to notice it. We can even feel it without looking at our belly. Want to try? Don't look at your belly, keep your head straight and put a hand on your belly. Just like this, with your hand, try to feel if your belly is going out or going in. "Oh, my belly is going out... Oh, my belly is going in..."

Then you can even try without touching your belly at all. Put your hands on your knees and try to feel inside your body if your belly is going out or going in. It's more tricky but with a little bit of practice, you can do it!

Sometimes we would like to do something, but we don't know what. So, we are bored. People don't like to be bored and not have anything to do. However, it is good for you to have little moments when you do nothing. It helps your head to rest a little, and resting is very important to grow up correctly when you are a child.

Your head is like an extraordinary machine. It's like a super computer that works all the time. But to keep working well, this machine needs to rest from time to time.

Your head rests at night when you sleep. That's why it's important to sleep well at night.

But your head can also rest a little bit during the day, during the moments when you do nothing.

To meditate is to do nothing on purpose. It can be very nice and fun. To be bored is to do nothing because you don't know what to do, and it's not nice or fun. That's why meditating and being bored are not exactly the same thing. However, sometimes, when we meditate, it happens that we find it boring.

That's why, when you meditate, it's good to remind yourself that although it can be a little bit boring, it is good for you. When you meditate, you help your head to rest and it helps you to grow up well.

And, on days when we do nothing because we don't know what to do...
On days when we are bored...

We can tell ourselves : "Hey, instead of being bored, what if I meditate?"

The end

In loving memory of my Dharma brother
Chris 'Kwan Haeng' Cheney
Bodhisattva teacher & meditator cat

THANK YOU:
to Marie Welch & Ben Hayes
to Zen Master Jok Um
and to the whole Kwan Um family